Contents

What is a mountain?

A mountain is a rocky, tall **landform**.

Mountains are very large.

Different types of plants and animals live in the mountains.

There are **non-living** things in the mountains, too.

What are living things?

Living things are alive. Living things need air and **sunlight**. Living things need food and water.

Living things grow and change.

Living things move on their own.

What are non-living things?

Non-living things are not alive. Non-living things do not need air and **sunlight**.

Non-living things do not need food or water.

Non-living things do not grow and change on their own.

Non-living things do not move on their own.

Is a pine tree living or non-living?

A pine tree needs water.

A pine tree moves on its own towards the sun.

A pine tree grows and changes.

A pine tree needs air and **sunlight**.

A pine tree is **living**.

Is ice living or non-living?

Ice does not move on its own.

Ice does not grow.

Ice does not need food.

Ice does not need air or **sunlight**.

Ice is **non-living**.

Is a mountain lion living or non-living?

A mountain lion grows and changes.

A mountain lion needs food and water.

A mountain lion moves on its own.

A mountain lion needs air and **sunlight**.

A mountain lion is **living**.

Is soil living or non-living?

Soil does not move on its own.

Soil does not need food or water.

Soil does not grow on its own.

Soil does not need air or **sunlight**.

Soil is **non-living**.

Is an eagle living or non-living?

An eagle grows and changes.

An eagle needs food and water.

An eagle moves on its own.

An eagle needs air and **sunlight**.

An eagle is **living**.

Is a wild flower living or non-living?

A wild flower moves on its own towards the sun.

A wild flower needs water.

A wild flower grows and changes.

A wild flower needs air and **sunlight**.

A wild flower is **living**.

What do you think?

Is this rock **living** or **non-living**?

Glossary

landform natural shape in the land

living alive. Living things need food and water. They breathe and move on their own. They grow and change.

non-living not alive. Non-living things do not need food or water. They do not move on their own. They do not grow and change on their own.

sunlight light from the sun

Find out more

Websites

Click through these images of living and non-living things, then take a quiz!
www.bbc.co.uk/schools/scienceclips/ages/5_6/ourselves.shtml

Look for eight living things in this pond scene!
www.bbc.co.uk/schools/scienceclips/ages/8_9/habitats.shtml

Check out this site to learn more about what living things need.
www.kidsbiology.com/biology_basics/needs_living_things/living_things_have_needs1.php

Books

About Habitats: Mountains, Cathryn Sill (Peachtree Publishers, 2009)

Living and Nonliving, Carol K. Lindeen (Capstone Press, 2008)

Index